Sir Cumference and the Fracton Faire

A Math Adventure

Cindy Neuschwander

Illustrated by **Wayne Geehan**

■■■ Charlesbridge

For 5/5 of my grandchildren: Annika, Isaac, Ava, Rachel, and Scott. A whole lot of thanks to my amazing editor, Yolanda Scott.—C. N.

To Chatham, Logan, and Luke Wood, with love.—W. G.

Published by Charlesbridge
85 Main Street
Watertown, MA 02472
(617) 926-0329
www.charlesbridge.com

Library of Congress Cataloging-in-Publication Data
Names: Neuschwander, Cindy, author. | Geehan, Wayne, illustrator.
Title: Sir Cumference and the Fracton Faire / Cindy Neuschwander ;
    illustrated by Wayne Geehan.
Description: Watertown, MA : Charlesbridge, [2017] | Description based
    on print version record and CIP data provided by publisher; resource not viewed.
Identifiers: LCCN 2015045100 (print) | LCCN 2015043914 (ebook)
    | ISBN 9781607348504 (ebook) | ISBN 9781607348511 (ebook pdf)
    | ISBN 9781570917714 (reinforced for library use)
    | ISBN 9781570917721 (softcover)
Subjects: LCSH: Fractions—Juvenile literature. | Mathematics—Juvenile literature.
Classification: LCC QA117 (print) | LCC QA117 .N48 2017 (ebook)
    | DDC 513.2/6—dc23
LC record available at http://lccn.loc.gov/2015045100

Printed in China
(hc) 10 9 8 7 6 5 4 3 2 1
(sc) 10 9 8 7 6 5 4 3 2 1

Illustrations done in acrylic paint on canvas
Display type set in Caslon LT Std Antique by Linotype
Text type set in Dante MT by Monotype
Color separations by Colourscan Print Co Pte Ltd, Singapore
Printed by 1010 Printing International Limited in Huizhou,
    Guangdong, China
Production supervision by Brian G. Walker
Designed by Martha MacLeod Sikkema

"Fine fabrics!" "Fresh cheese!" *Baa, baa!*

It was the opening morning of the Fracton Faire.

"Such a merry atmosphere!" said Lady Di of Ameter. She and Sir Cumference strolled jauntily through the crowds with their friend Reginald Parton, the Earl of Fracton.

3

The two men stopped to watch a sword swallower while Lady Di wandered over to a cloth merchant's booth. She ran her hand over a length of fabric. "How perfectly soft!" she exclaimed.

The merchant smiled. "You can buy all or part," she said, pointing to the sign above her.

"What do those numbers mean?" Lady Di asked.

"They're Fracton numbers, my lady," the woman answered. "They are used to measure equal pieces of something, such as this beautiful cloth."

"Why is one number below the other?" asked Lady Di.

"The bottom number is called the *denominator,*" the seller explained. "It shows how many parts are in a whole."

She drew lines on the material with a soap sliver, dividing the fabric into equal sections.

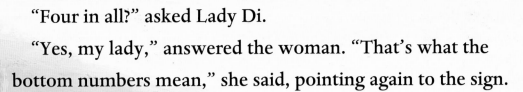

"Four in all?" asked Lady Di.

"Yes, my lady," answered the woman. "That's what the bottom numbers mean," she said, pointing again to the sign.

"And if I want just one part of the four?" asked Lady Di.

"The *numerator*, or top number, tells me how many parts of the cloth you want. In this case it would be one," said the woman.

Lady Di printed the Fracton number ¼ on the first section of the cloth.

"Indeed! That's one-fourth," replied the merchant. "And two parts of the four would be two-fourths; three parts of the four are three-fourths; and the entire length is four-fourths; or one whole."

Lady Di smiled. "I'm partial to red fabric. Have you any?"
The merchant nodded and bent down. "Odd . . . my red
material seems to be missing. I'm so sorry, my lady." She
excused herself and hurried away to check with neighboring
cloth sellers.

At this point, Sir Cumference and the earl approached, each hungry enough to eat half a horse.

"Soft curds here!" bellowed a portly cheese monger. "Wheels of cheese! Parts or whole."

"I'll take one-half of that Wensleydale wheel," said the earl.

"I'd like two-fourths of that Cheshire wheel," said Lady Di. She thought of her lesson on numerators. Two pieces meant she could save one for later.

"I'm so hungry I'll have . . . this much of the Stilton!" said Sir Cumference, pointing to four-eighths on the sign. He thought the bigger numbers meant more cheese. But when the portions were cut, they were the same amount.

"They're equivalent," explained the cheese monger. "The Stilton is cut into smaller pieces, so there are more of them. Here, I'll cut the cheddar wheel and you'll see. . . . Wait a tick! Where is it?"

Missing cheese? Lady Di remembered the missing red cloth. Was it just a coincidence?

Tucked away from the hubbub, six men were divvying up a round of tangy cheddar and looking over a pile of other stolen goods from the faire.

"Well done, lads!" Bad Old Barnaby said to his brigand band. "We've pinched some right proper stuff, we have!"

Spread out beside them were meats, breads, ale, yarn,
fabric, purses, coins, and four fluffy sheep.

"That cloth was the easiest pickings I ever did pilfer!"
chortled one of Barnaby's men.

By now almost everyone at the faire was missing something.
People surrounded the earl, all talking at once.

The earl's head sheep shearer pushed forward.

"My lord!" he exclaimed. "One-third of your finest sheep
are missing. We had a dozen to clip, but four are gone!"

"Thieves!" growled the earl. "They desire easy gain.
Let's think like a thief so we can catch the culprit."

A plan was quickly hatched.

"It's a long shot, but it might work. Our puppeteer will set the trap," the earl said, "and Fracton numbers will do nine-tenths of the work."

At high noon the performance began. It featured Fracton's two favorite puppets, the diminutive Half-Pint and the sizable Pottle.

The audience roared with laughter.

"You got that right!" Barnaby snickered, poking one of his mates in the ribs. The brigand band had returned to enjoy the performance.

The audience sprang into action. A gold sovereign was enough money to buy a small farm.

"The thief will want that coin," the earl said to Sir Cumference and Lady Di. "We had no stealing before the faire began, so we think the thief is an outsider to Fracton."

"And you wager that an outsider would think a number like that one-sixteenth is bigger than something like one-third because the denominator is larger," said Lady Di.

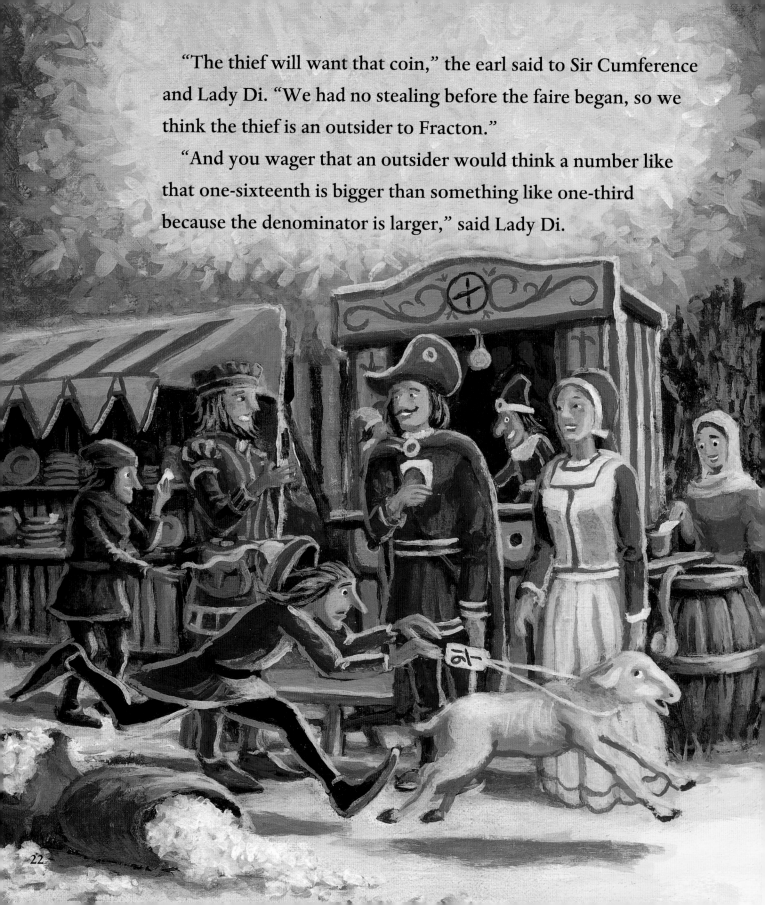

"I made that mistake myself," admitted Sir Cumference. "Now I realize that the larger the denominator, the smaller each part is. The higher the numerator, the more parts there are."

People were having fun searching. Fracton numbers were discovered in unusual places.

A small girl noticed a ⁷⁄₉ between two slices of bread. "This could be the winning number!" she said excitedly.

Barnaby and his band kept their eyes peeled for Fracton numbers. They observed a woman unwrapping a ½ from around a wool wax jar, but they dismissed it.

"Too small," Barnaby told his men.

A young boy and his father spotted a $\frac{1}{32}$ slip.

"Such a tiny Fracton number," moaned the boy.

"Leave it, son," his father said. "No one would be stupid enough to want that." They left it on a lunch table, where Barnaby took it.

"Ho ho, lads!" he chuckled. "We're in luck now, we are!
Big numbers! This must be the winning ticket."

The tower bells rang at half-past two.

"Would everyone with a slip step forward?" the earl asked the crowd. "And please line up by number size."

"I'm here in the middle," said the woman with ½.

"Mine's a bit larger than one-half," said a boy with ⅝.

"This one is larger still, I think," said the little girl with 7/9. The slip holders jostled about, but finally everyone was in order, with Barnaby proudly standing on one end with 1/32 and sweet little Madeline Elizabeth Holparte on the other with 1/1.

"The gentleman with *one thirty-second*!" called the puppet master. "As the holder of the smallest Fracton number, you may award the golden coin to the winner, who holds the *one whole* slip."

"No!" screeched Barnaby. "My number is biggest! The coin's mine!" He ran toward the gold sovereign. The earl blocked him. Defeated, Barnaby and his brigand band turned and fled.

"They were too fast," the earl said, returning to the puppet
theater after a fruitless chase. "But we found the stolen goods."

"Those half-dozen ruffians were a whole heap of trouble!"
said Sir Cumference.

"But they fell to pieces in the end!" exclaimed the earl happily.

The village of Fracton and its earl continued to be famous for sheep, the faire, and the unique way they wrote their numbers. Those numbers became known as *fractons* in Angleland. People used them when they wanted to represent parts of things. Today we call them *fractions*.